cool cupcakes

THE AUSTRALIAN
Women's Weekly

CONTENTS

AUSTRALIAN CUP AND
SPOON MEASUREMENTS
ARE METRIC.
A CONVERSION CHART
APPEARS ON PAGE 77.

These fabulous recipes will impress all your family and friends. Once you have tried them, you will never bake a boring old cupcake again. It's important to follow the recipe when you're baking. Take your time and you will succeed.

Pamela Clark

Food Director

BLUE RIBBONS

prep + cook time **1 hour** makes **12**

choc-orange almond cakes

60g (2 ounces) dark (semi-sweet) eating chocolate, chopped coarsely
1 teaspoon finely grated orange rind
⅔ cup (160ml) orange juice
90g (3 ounces) butter, softened
1 cup (220g) firmly packed light brown sugar
2 eggs
⅔ cup (100g) self-raising flour
2 tablespoons cocoa powder
⅓ cup (40g) ground almonds

decorations

½ cup (80g) icing (confectioners') sugar
375g (12 ounces) ready-made white icing
blue food colouring
⅓ cup (110g) orange marmalade, warmed, strained
8cm (3-inch) round cutter
2m (80 inches) ribbon, approximately

1 Preheat oven to 170°C/340°F. Line 12-hole (⅓-cup/80ml) muffin pan with paper cases.

2 Combine chocolate, rind and juice in small saucepan; stir over low heat until mixture is smooth.

3 Beat butter, sugar and eggs in small bowl with electric mixer until light and fluffy. Stir in sifted flour and cocoa, ground almonds and warm chocolate mixture. Divide mixture into paper cases; smooth tops.

4 Bake about 25 minutes. Stand cakes in pan 5 minutes before turning, top-side up, onto wire rack to cool.

5 Dust work surface with sifted icing sugar; knead ready-made icing until smooth. Knead blue colouring into icing.

6 Brush cold cakes with marmalade. Roll icing out to 5mm (¼-inch) thickness. Using round cutter, cut 12 rounds from icing. Place rounds on cakes; tie cakes with ribbon.

tip **This recipe also makes 6 texas muffins (¾-cup/180ml); bake about 35 minutes.**

2

CHOCOLATE HEARTS

prep + cook time **1 hour (+ standing)** makes **18**

dark chocolate mud cakes

30g (1 ounce) dark (semi-sweet) eating chocolate, chopped coarsely
⅓ cup (80ml) water
45g (1½ ounces) butter, softened
½ cup (110g) firmly packed light brown sugar
1 egg
⅓ cup (50g) self-raising flour
1 tablespoon cocoa powder
2 tablespoons ground almonds

decorations

100g (3 ounces) white chocolate Melts, melted
2cm (¾-inch) heart-shaped cutter

butter cream

90g (3 ounces) butter, softened
1 cup (240g) icing (confectioners') sugar
1 tablespoon milk
pink and blue food colouring

1 Preheat oven to 170°C/340°F. Line 18 holes of two 12-hole (1-tablespoon/20ml) mini muffin pans with paper cases.
2 Stir chocolate and the water in small saucepan over low heat until smooth.
3 Beat butter, sugar and egg in small bowl with electric mixer until light and fluffy. Stir in sifted flour and cocoa, ground almonds and warm chocolate mixture. Drop level tablespoons of mixture into each paper case.
4 Bake about 15 minutes. Stand cakes in pans 5 minutes before turning, top-side up, onto wire racks to cool.
5 Meanwhile, make white chocolate heart decorations by spreading a thin layer of the melted chocolate over a sheet of baking paper; stand chocolate at room temperature until set. Using heart-shaped cutter, cut 18 hearts from chocolate.
6 Make butter cream. Dollop tops of half the cold cakes with generous spoonfuls of pink butter cream; dollop the tops of remaining cakes with generous spoonfuls of blue butter cream. Gently push hearts into butter cream.
butter cream Beat butter in small bowl with electric mixer until as white as possible; beat in sifted icing sugar and milk, in two batches. Divide butter cream between two small bowls; tint one bowl pale pink and the other pale blue with colouring.

BUTTON UPS

prep + cook time **1 hour** makes **18**

carrot cakes

1 cup (250ml) vegetable oil
1⅓ cups (300g) firmly packed light brown sugar
3 eggs
3 cups firmly packed, coarsely grated carrot
1 cup (110g) coarsely chopped walnuts
2½ cups (375g) self-raising flour
½ teaspoon bicarbonate of soda (baking soda)
2 teaspoons mixed spice

decorations

½ cup (80g) icing (confectioners') sugar
250g (8 ounces) ready-made white icing
yellow food colouring
⅓ cup (110g) apricot jam, warmed, strained
8cm (3-inch) round cutter
6cm (2¼-inch) round cutter
72 mini mints

1 Preheat oven to 180°C/350°F. Line 18 holes of two 12-hole (⅓-cup/80ml) muffin pans with paper cases.

2 Beat oil, sugar and eggs in small bowl with electric mixer until thick. Transfer mixture to large bowl; stir in carrot, nuts, then sifted dry ingredients. Drop ¼ cups of mixture into paper cases.

3 Bake about 30 minutes. Stand cakes in pans 5 minutes before turning, top-side up, onto wire racks to cool.

4 Dust work surface with sifted icing sugar; knead ready-made icing until smooth. Knead yellow colouring into icing.

5 Brush cold cakes with a little jam. Roll icing between sheets of baking paper until 5mm (¼ inch) thick. Using cutter, cut 18 x 8cm (3-inch) rounds from the icing; position rounds on cakes. Use the blunt edge of 6cm (2¼-inch) round cutter to mark the edge of the buttons. Position mini mints to make button holes.

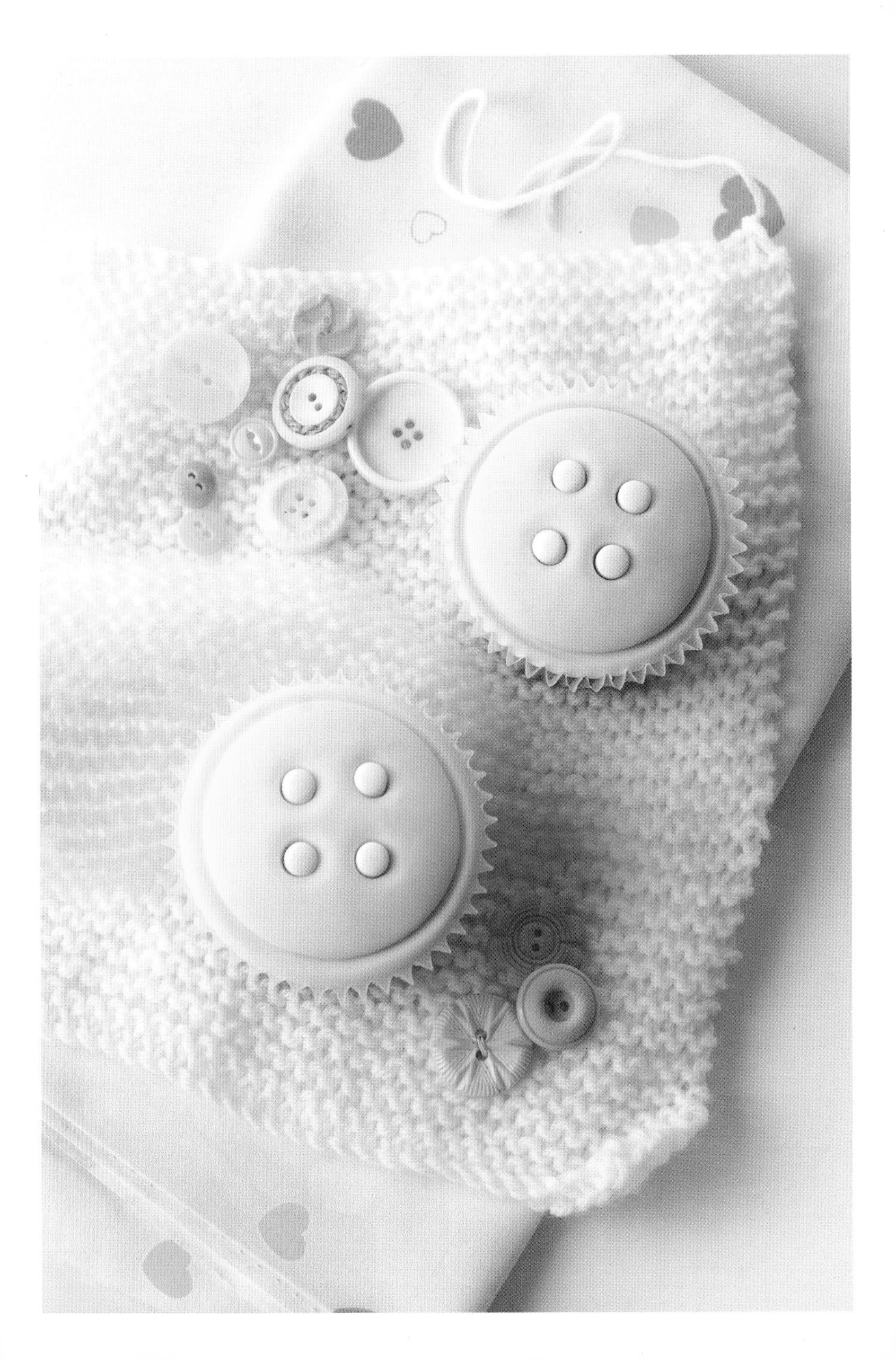

COCONUT ICE BUTTERFLIES

prep + cook time **1 hour** makes **8**

coconut butter cakes

90g (3 ounces) butter, softened
1 teaspoon coconut extract
½ cup (110g) caster (superfine) sugar
2 eggs
1 cup (150g) self-raising flour
2 tablespoons milk

pink glacé icing

2 cups (320g) icing (confectioners') sugar
1 teaspoon softened butter
2 tablespoons hot water, approximately
pink food colouring

decorations

½ cup (40g) desiccated coconut
¼ cup (80g) strawberry jam
½ cup (125ml) thickened (heavy) cream, whipped

1 Preheat oven to 180°C/350°F. Line eight holes of 12-hole (⅓-cup/80ml) muffin pan with paper cases.
2 Beat butter, extract, sugar, eggs, sifted flour and milk in small bowl with electric mixer on low speed until ingredients are combined. Increase speed to medium; beat until mixture has changed to a paler colour. Drop ¼ cups of mixture into paper cases.
3 Bake about 20 minutes. Stand cakes in pan 5 minutes before turning, top-side up, onto wire rack to cool.
4 Make pink glacé icing.
5 Place coconut in small shallow bowl. Working with one cake at a time, spread (or dip) tops of cold cakes with icing, then immediately dip each in coconut. Stand cakes on wire rack to set.
6 Cut a round hole, about 1cm (½ inch) deep, in the top of each cake. Halve rounds to make butterfly wings. Fill each hole with jam and cream. Position the wings on cakes.
pink glacé icing Sift icing sugar into small heatproof bowl; stir in butter and enough of the hot water to make a thick paste. Stir over small saucepan of simmering water until icing is spreadable. Tint icing pink with food colouring.

tip **Tie a small pink ribbon in a bow around each cake, if you like.**

ROCKY ROAD CAKES

prep + cook time **45 minutes** makes **12**

marble cakes

125g (4 ounces) butter, softened
½ teaspoon vanilla extract
⅔ cup (150g) caster (superfine) sugar
2 eggs
1¼ cups (185g) self-raising flour
⅓ cup (80ml) milk
pink food colouring
1 tablespoon cocoa powder
2 teaspoons milk, extra

rocky road topping

½ cup (70g) roasted unsalted peanuts
1 cup (200g) red glacé cherries, halved
1 cup (100g) pink and white marshmallows, chopped coarsely
½ cup (25g) flaked coconut, toasted
200g (6½ ounces) milk eating chocolate, melted

decorations

60g (2 ounces) milk chocolate Melts, melted

1 Preheat oven to 180°C/350°F. Line 12-hole (⅓-cup/80ml) muffin pan with paper cases.
2 Beat butter, extract, sugar and eggs in small bowl with electric mixer until light and fluffy. Stir in sifted flour and milk, in two batches.
3 Divide mixture evenly between three bowls. Tint one mixture pink. Blend sifted cocoa with extra milk in a cup; stir into second mixture. Leave third mixture plain.
4 Drop alternate spoonfuls of mixtures into paper cases. Pull a skewer backwards and forwards through mixtures to create a marbled effect; smooth surface.
5 Bake about 20 minutes. Stand cakes in pan 5 minutes before turning, top-side up, onto wire rack to cool.
6 Make rocky road topping.
7 Place topping on tops of cold cakes; position plain nuts, cherries, marshmallows and coconut on top, pressing into chocolate before it sets. Drizzle the melted chocolate over topping, to decorate.

rocky road topping Combine about two-thirds of the nuts, cherries, marshmallow and coconut with melted chocolate in medium bowl. Leave remaining nuts, cherries, marshmallows and coconut plain.

tip **This recipe also makes 6 texas muffins (¾-cup/180ml); bake about 30 minutes.**

MOSAIC MAGIC

prep + cook time **1 hour (+ cooling & standing)** makes **12**

caramel mud cakes

125g (4 ounces) butter, chopped coarsely
100g (3½ ounces) white eating chocolate, chopped coarsely
⅔ cup (150g) firmly packed light brown sugar
¼ cup (90g) golden syrup (or treacle)
⅔ cup (160ml) milk
1 cup (150g) plain (all-purpose) flour
⅓ cup (50g) self-raising flour
1 egg

white chocolate ganache

½ cup (125ml) pouring cream
345g (11 ounces) white eating chocolate, chopped coarsely

decorations

blue and green lollies

1 Preheat oven to 170°C/340°F. Line 12-hole (⅓-cup/80ml) muffin pan with paper cases.
2 Stir butter, chocolate, sugar, syrup and milk in small saucepan over low heat until smooth. Transfer mixture to medium bowl; cool 15 minutes.
3 Whisk sifted flours into chocolate mixture, then whisk in egg. Drop ¼ cups of mixture into paper cases.
4 Bake about 30 minutes. Stand cakes in pan 5 minutes before turning, top-side up, onto wire rack to cool.
5 Meanwhile, make white chocolate ganache.
6 Spread cold cakes thickly with ganache. Decorate each cake in a mosaic pattern with blue and green lollies, gently pushing the lollies into the ganache.

white chocolate ganache Bring cream to the boil in small saucepan; remove from heat. When bubbles subside, add chocolate; stir until smooth. Cover; stand at room temperature 15 minutes or until ganache is spreadable.

tip **We used blue and green Lifesavers, mini M&M's, Skittles and baby jelly beans, but you can use any lollies you like.**

PEPPERMINT SUNDAES

prep + cook time **45 minutes** makes **15**

quick-mix chocolate cakes
1 cup (150g) self-raising flour
½ cup (75g) plain (all-purpose) flour
⅓ cup (35g) cocoa powder
¾ cup (165g) caster (superfine) sugar
185g (6 ounces) butter, softened
3 eggs
½ cup (125ml) milk
peppermint butter cream
125g (4 ounces) butter, softened
1 teaspoon peppermint extract
1½ cups (240g) icing (confectioners') sugar
2 tablespoons milk
green food colouring
decorations
2 x 30g (1-ounce) Flake chocolate bars, crumbled
185g (6 ounces) milk chocolate Melts, melted

1 Preheat oven to 180°C/350°F. Line 15 holes of two 12-hole (⅓-cup/80ml) muffin pans with paper cases.
2 Sift dry ingredients into medium bowl, add remaining ingredients; beat with electric mixer on low speed until combined. Increase speed to medium; beat until mixture is smooth and changed to a paler colour. Drop ¼ cups of mixture into paper cases.
3 Bake about 20 minutes. Stand cakes in pans 5 minutes before turning, top-side up, onto wire racks to cool.
4 Make peppermint butter cream. Stir half the Flake through the butter cream.
5 Dollop a generous amount of butter cream onto a cold cake then use a spatula to form it into the rounded shape of a scoop of ice-cream. Spoon some melted chocolate over the butter cream then sprinkle with more crumbled Flake before the chocolate sets. Repeat with remaining cakes.
peppermint butter cream Beat butter and extract in small bowl with electric mixer until as white as possible; beat in sifted icing sugar and milk, in two batches. Tint butter cream pale green with colouring.

FRANGIPANI ROSEWATER CAKES

prep + cook time **55 minutes (+ cooling)** makes **8**

rosewater cakes

90g (3 ounces) butter, softened
1 tablespoon rosewater
½ cup (110g) caster (superfine) sugar
2 eggs
1 cup (150g) self-raising flour
2 tablespoons milk

fluffy mock cream

2 tablespoons milk
⅓ cup (80ml) water
1 cup (220g) caster (superfine) sugar
1 teaspoon gelatine
2 tablespoons water, extra
250g (8 ounces) butter, softened
½ teaspoon vanilla extract

decorations

20 white marshmallows
pink sugar sprinkles

1 Preheat oven to 180°C/350°F. Line eight holes of 12-hole (⅓-cup/80ml) muffin pan with paper cases.
2 Beat butter, rosewater, sugar, eggs, sifted flour and milk in small bowl with electric mixer on low speed until combined. Increase speed to medium; beat until mixture has changed to a paler colour. Drop ¼ cups of mixture into paper cases.
3 Bake about 20 minutes. Stand cakes in pan 5 minutes before turning, top-side up, onto wire rack to cool.
4 Make fluffy mock cream; spoon into a large piping bag fitted with a large fluted tube. Pipe stars on top of each cake.
5 Cut marshmallows in half horizontally; dip sticky sides into pink sugar sprinkles. Pinch one end of each marshmallow-half to make a petal shape. Use five halves to make each frangipani, using more pink sprinkles to fill in any white gaps on the marshmallows.
fluffy mock cream Combine milk, the water and sugar in small saucepan; stir over low heat, without boiling, until sugar is dissolved. Sprinkle gelatine over extra water in cup, add to pan; stir syrup until gelatine is dissolved. Cool mixture to room temperature. Beat butter and extract in small bowl with electric mixer until as white as possible. While motor is operating, gradually pour in cold syrup; beat until light and fluffy. The mixture will thicken on standing.

SEQUIN SWIRLS

prep + cook time **50 minutes (+ cooling)** makes **12**

white chocolate mud cakes

125g (4 ounces) butter, chopped coarsely
75g (2½ ounces) white eating chocolate, chopped coarsely
1 cup (220g) caster (superfine) sugar
½ cup (125ml) milk
½ cup (75g) plain (all-purpose) flour
½ cup (75g) self-raising flour
1 egg

fluffy frosting

1 cup (220g) caster (superfine) sugar
⅓ cup (80ml) water
2 egg whites

decorations

edible sequins

1 Preheat oven to 170°C/340°F. Line 12-hole (⅓-cup/80ml) muffin pan with paper cases.
2 Stir butter, chocolate, sugar and milk in small saucepan over low heat until smooth. Transfer mixture to medium bowl; cool 15 minutes.
3 Whisk sifted flours into chocolate mixture, then whisk in egg. Drop ¼ cups of mixture into paper cases.
4 Bake about 30 minutes. Stand cakes in pan 5 minutes before turning, top-side up, onto wire rack to cool.
5 Make fluffy frosting. Spoon frosting into large piping bag fitted with a large fluted tube. Pipe a large swirl of frosting on cake tops; sprinkle cakes with edible sequins.
fluffy frosting Combine sugar and the water in small saucepan; stir over heat, without boiling, until sugar is dissolved. Bring to the boil; boil, uncovered, without stirring, about 5 minutes or until syrup reaches 116°C/245°F on a candy thermometer. Syrup should be thick but not coloured. Remove from heat, allow bubbles to subside. Beat egg whites in small bowl with electric mixer until soft peaks form. While motor is operating, add hot syrup in a thin steady stream; beat on high speed about 10 minutes or until mixture is thick.

tip **If you don't have a candy thermometer, boil the syrup until it's thick with heavy bubbles. Remove from heat, let bubbles subside, then reassess the thickness of the syrup.**

BANANA CARAMEL CAKES

prep + cook time **55 minutes** makes **12**

sour cream banana cakes

90g (3 ounces) butter, softened
½ cup (110g) firmly packed light brown sugar
2 eggs
½ cup (75g) self-raising flour
½ cup (75g) plain (all-purpose) flour
½ teaspoon bicarbonate of soda (baking soda)
½ teaspoon mixed spice
⅔ cup mashed overripe banana
⅓ cup (80g) sour cream
2 tablespoons milk

caramel banana filling

375g (12 ounces) canned Top 'n' Fill caramel
½ cup (125ml) thickened (heavy) cream, whipped
2 medium bananas (400g), sliced thinly
100g (3½ ounces) dark (semi-sweet) eating chocolate

1 Preheat oven to 180°C/350°F. Line 12-hole (⅓-cup/80ml) muffin pan with paper cases.
2 Beat butter, sugar and eggs in small bowl with electric mixer until light and fluffy. Stir in sifted dry ingredients, banana, sour cream and milk. Divide mixture into paper cases; smooth surface.
3 Bake about 20 minutes. Stand cakes in pan 5 minutes before turning, top-side up, onto wire rack to cool. Remove paper cases from cold cakes.
4 Fold 2 tablespoons of the caramel into cream.
5 Cut cakes horizontally into three slices. Re-assemble cakes with remaining caramel and sliced banana. Top cakes with caramel-flavoured cream.
6 Using a vegetable peeler, grate chocolate; sprinkle over cake tops.

tips **This recipe also makes 6 texas muffins (¾-cup/180ml); bake about 25 minutes. Two large (460g) overripe bananas will give 1 cup mashed banana.**

CHOC-HONEYCOMB GINGER CAKES

prep + cook time **55 minutes** makes **12**

90g (3 ounces) butter, softened
1 egg
¼ cup (60ml) buttermilk
2 tablespoons golden syrup (or treacle)
½ cup (110g) firmly packed light brown sugar
½ cup (75g) plain (all-purpose) flour
½ cup (75g) self-raising flour
¼ teaspoon bicarbonate of soda (baking soda)
1 teaspoon ground ginger
½ teaspoon ground cinnamon
¼ teaspoon ground nutmeg
45g (1½ ounces) dark (semi-sweet) eating chocolate, chopped coarsely

decorations

1¼ cups (310ml) thickened (heavy) cream
3 x 45g (1½ ounces) Violet Crumble bars, chopped coarsely

1 Preheat oven to 170°C/340°F. Line 12-hole (⅓-cup/80ml) muffin pan with paper cases.

2 Beat butter, egg, buttermilk, syrup and sifted dry ingredients in small bowl with electric mixer on low speed until combined. Increase speed to medium; beat until mixture has changed to a paler colour. Stir chocolate into mixture. Divide into paper cases; smooth surface.

3 Bake about 30 minutes. Stand cakes in pan 5 minutes before turning, top-side up, onto wire rack to cool.

4 Spread cold cakes with whipped cream; top with chopped Violet Crumble.

tips **It is fine to use just one 300ml carton of cream for this recipe. This recipe also makes 6 texas muffins (¾-cup/180ml); bake about 40 minutes.**

CAKEUCCINOS

prep + cook time **45 minutes (+ cooling)** makes **15**

quick-mix chocolate cakes

185g (6 ounces) butter, softened
¾ cup (165g) caster (superfine) sugar
3 eggs
½ cup (125ml) milk
1 cup (150g) self-raising flour
½ cup (75g) plain (all-purpose) flour
⅓ cup (35g) cocoa powder

fluffy mock cream

2 tablespoons milk
⅓ cup (80ml) water
1 cup (220g) caster (superfine) sugar
1 teaspoon gelatine
2 tablespoons water, extra
250g (8 ounces) butter, softened
½ teaspoon vanilla extract

decorations

cappuccino stencil (see tip)
½ cup (50g) cocoa powder

1 Preheat oven to 180°C/350°F. Line 15 holes of two 12-hole (⅓-cup/80ml) muffin pans with paper cases.

2 Beat butter, sugar, eggs, milk and sifted dry ingredients in medium bowl with electric mixer on low speed until combined. Increase speed to medium; beat until mixture is smooth and changed to a paler colour. Drop ¼ cups of mixture into paper cases.

3 Bake about 20 minutes. Stand cakes in pans 5 minutes before turning, top-side up, onto wire racks to cool.

4 Make fluffy mock cream. Spread cold cakes with mock cream. Working with one cake at a time, hold stencil close to the top of the cake. Use a fine sifter to sift cocoa powder over stencil. Gently lift the stencil away from the cake. Brush away any excess cocoa from the stencil before using on the next cake.

fluffy mock cream Combine milk, the water and sugar in small saucepan; stir over low heat, without boiling, until sugar is dissolved. Sprinkle gelatine over extra water in cup, add to pan; stir syrup until gelatine is dissolved. Cool mixture to room temperature. Beat butter and extract in small bowl with electric mixer until as white as possible. While motor is operating, gradually pour in cold syrup; beat until mixture is light and fluffy. Mixture will thicken on standing.

tip **Stencils are available from cake decorating suppliers and craft stores.**

COCONUT CHERRY TOPS

prep + cook time **45 minutes** makes **8**

coconut butter cakes

90g (3 ounces) butter, softened
1 teaspoon coconut extract
½ cup (110g) caster (superfine) sugar
2 eggs
1 cup (150g) self-raising flour
2 tablespoons milk

cream cheese frosting

60g (2 ounces) butter, softened
155g (5 ounces) cream cheese, softened
3 cups (480g) icing (confectioners') sugar

decorations

2 tablespoons desiccated coconut
8 maraschino cherries

1 Preheat oven to 180°C/350°F. Line eight holes of 12-hole (⅓-cup/80ml) muffin pan with paper cases.
2 Beat butter, extract, sugar, eggs, sifted flour and milk in small bowl with electric mixer on low speed until ingredients are combined. Increase speed to medium; beat until mixture has changed to a paler colour. Drop ¼ cups of mixture into paper cases.
3 Bake about 20 minutes. Stand cakes in pan 5 minutes before turning, top-side up, onto wire rack to cool.
4 Make cream cheese frosting.
5 Spoon frosting into large piping bag fitted with a large fluted tube. Pipe a large swirl of frosting on the top of each cake; sprinkle lightly with desiccated coconut, top with a maraschino cherry.
cream cheese frosting Beat butter and cream cheese in small bowl with electric mixer until light and fluffy; gradually beat in sifted icing sugar.

tip **Maraschino cherries are cherries that have been soaked, flavoured and often coloured, resulting in a sweet, bright, glossy fruit, perfect for garnish. They can be bought in jars at most supermarkets, greengrocers and specialty food shops.**

GLAMOUR MASKS

prep + cook time **1 hour 10 minutes (+ cooling)** makes **12**

white chocolate mud cakes

125g (4 ounces) butter, chopped coarsely
75g (2½ ounces) white eating chocolate, chopped coarsely
1 cup (220g) caster (superfine) sugar
½ cup (125ml) milk
½ cup (75g) plain (all-purpose) flour
½ cup (75g) self-raising flour
1 egg

butter cream

125g (4 ounces) butter, softened
1½ cups (240g) icing (confectioners') sugar
2 tablespoons milk
blue food colouring

decorations

silver and blue cachous
12 lollipop sticks
1.5m (60 inches) blue ribbon
12 blue edible sugar flowers

1 Preheat oven to 170°C/340°F. Line 12-hole (⅓-cup/80ml) muffin pan with paper cases.
2 Stir butter, chocolate, sugar and milk in small saucepan over low heat until smooth. Transfer mixture to medium bowl; cool 15 minutes.
3 Whisk sifted flours into chocolate mixture, then whisk in egg. Drop ¼ cups of mixture into paper cases.
4 Bake about 30 minutes. Stand cakes in pan 5 minutes before turning, top-side up, onto wire rack to cool.
5 Make butter cream. Spread cold cakes with butter cream.
6 Make a mask shape on each cake using silver and blue cachous. Push cachous gently into butter cream. Use sticks cut from lollipops for the handles of the masks. Use small pieces of ribbon and sugar flowers to cover and decorate the tops of the handles.
butter cream Beat butter in small bowl with electric mixer until as white as possible; beat in sifted icing sugar and milk, in two batches. Tint butter cream blue with food colouring.

MALT GANACHE SWIRLS

prep + cook time **50 minutes (+ refrigeration)** makes **15**

quick-mix chocolate cakes

185g (6 ounces) butter, softened
¾ cup (165g) caster (superfine) sugar
3 eggs
½ cup (125ml) milk
1 cup (150g) self-raising flour
½ cup (75g) plain (all-purpose) flour
⅓ cup (35g) cocoa powder

whipped milk chocolate ganache

1 cup (250ml) pouring cream
410g (13 ounces) milk eating chocolate, chopped coarsely

decorations

brown mini M&M's
280g (9 ounces) Maltesers
gold cachous
gold edible glitter

1 Preheat oven to 180°C/350°F. Line 15 holes of two 12-hole (⅓-cup/80ml) muffin pans with paper cases.

2 Beat butter, sugar, eggs, milk and sifted flours and cocoa in medium bowl with electric mixer on low speed until ingredients are combined. Increase speed to medium; beat until mixture is smooth and has changed to a paler colour. Drop ¼ cups of mixture into paper cases.

3 Bake about 20 minutes. Stand cakes in pans 5 minutes before turning, top-side up, onto wire racks to cool.

4 Make whipped milk chocolate ganache. Spoon ganache into large piping bag fitted with a large fluted tube. Pipe generous swirls of ganache onto cold cakes; decorate with M&M's, Maltesers, gold cachous and edible glitter.

whipped milk chocolate ganache Bring cream to the boil in small saucepan; remove from heat. When bubbles subside, add chocolate; stir until smooth. Transfer mixture to small bowl. Cover; refrigerate 30 minutes. Beat with an electric mixer until light and fluffy.

tip **Edible glitter is available from cake decorating supply stores.**

RETORS D'ALSACE D·M·C
N° 30

MARBLED CHOC-CARAMEL CAKES

prep + cook time **1 hour (+ cooling & standing)** makes **12**

caramel mud cakes

125g (4 ounces) butter, chopped coarsely
100g (3½ ounces) white eating chocolate, chopped coarsely
⅔ cup (150g) firmly packed light brown sugar
¼ cup (90g) golden syrup (or treacle)
⅔ cup (160ml) milk
1 cup (150g) plain (all-purpose) flour
⅓ cup (50g) self-raising flour
1 egg

dark chocolate ganache

½ cup (125ml) pouring cream
200g (6½ ounces) dark (semi-sweet) eating chocolate, chopped coarsely

decorations

¾ cup (240g) caramel Top 'n' Fill

1 Preheat oven to 170°C/340°F. Line 12-hole (⅓-cup/80ml) muffin pan with paper cases.
2 Stir butter, chocolate, sugar, syrup and milk in small saucepan over low heat until smooth. Transfer mixture to medium bowl; cool 15 minutes.
3 Whisk sifted flours into chocolate mixture, then whisk in egg. Drop ¼ cups of mixture into paper cases.
4 Bake about 30 minutes. Stand cakes in pan 5 minutes before turning, top-side up, onto wire rack to cool.
5 Make dark chocolate ganache. Spread cold cakes with a thick layer of ganache; dollop about six small dots of caramel Top 'n' Fill on top of ganache. Pull a skewer back and forth through caramel for a marbled effect.
dark chocolate ganache Bring cream to the boil in small saucepan; remove from heat. When bubbles subside, add chocolate; stir until smooth. Cover; stand at room temperature 15 minutes or until ganache is spreadable.

MILK CHOC-HAZELNUT WHIPS

prep + cook time **50 minutes (+ refrigeration)** makes **9**

flourless choc-hazelnut cakes

¼ cup (25g) cocoa powder
¼ cup (60ml) hot water
100g (3½ ounces) dark (semi-sweet) eating chocolate, melted
100g (3½ ounces) butter, melted
1 cup (220g) firmly packed light brown sugar
¾ cup (75g) ground hazelnuts
3 eggs, separated

whipped milk chocolate ganache

¾ cup (180ml) pouring cream
315g (10 ounces) milk eating chocolate, chopped coarsely

decorations

2 tablespoons chocolate sprinkles

1 Preheat oven to 180°C/350°F. Line nine holes of 12-hole (⅓-cup/80ml) muffin pan with paper cases.

2 Blend cocoa with the water in medium bowl until smooth. Stir in chocolate, butter, sugar, nuts and egg yolks.

3 Beat egg whites in small bowl with electric mixer until soft peaks form; fold into chocolate mixture, in two batches. Pour ⅓ cups of mixture into paper cases.

4 Bake about 25 minutes. Stand cakes in pan 5 minutes before turning, top-side up, onto wire rack to cool.

5 Make whipped milk chocolate ganache. Spoon ganache into large piping bag fitted with a large fluted tube. Pipe large swirls of ganache onto cold cakes. Sprinkle with chocolate sprinkles.

whipped milk chocolate ganache Bring cream to the boil in small saucepan; remove from heat. When bubbles subside, add chocolate; stir until smooth. Transfer mixture to small bowl. Cover; refrigerate 30 minutes. Beat with an electric mixer until light and fluffy.

MARBLED CHOCOLATE MUD CAKES

prep + cook time **1 hour 5 minutes (+ standing)** makes **12**

dark chocolate mud cakes

90g (3 ounces) butter, chopped coarsely
75g (2½ ounces) dark (semi-sweet) eating chocolate, chopped coarsely
⅔ cup (150g) caster (superfine) sugar
½ cup (125ml) milk
½ cup (75g) plain (all-purpose) flour
¼ cup (35g) self-raising flour
1 tablespoon cocoa powder
1 egg

white chocolate mud cakes

90g (3 ounces) butter, chopped coarsely
75g (2½ ounces) white eating chocolate, chopped coarsely
½ cup (110g) caster (superfine) sugar
⅓ cup (80ml) milk
⅔ cup (100g) plain (all-purpose) flour
¼ cup (35g) self-raising flour
1 egg

dark chocolate ganache

⅓ cup (80ml) pouring cream
200g (6½ ounces) dark (semi-sweet) eating chocolate, chopped coarsely

white chocolate ganache

2 tablespoons pouring cream
100g (3½ ounces) white eating chocolate, chopped coarsely

1 Preheat oven to 160°C/325°F. Grease two six-hole (¾-cup/180ml) texas muffin pans.

2 Make dark chocolate mud cake by combining butter, chocolate, sugar and milk in medium saucepan; stir over low heat until smooth. Transfer to medium bowl; cool 10 minutes. Whisk in sifted flours and cocoa, then whisk in egg.

3 Make white chocolate mud cake by combining butter, chocolate, sugar and milk in medium saucepan; stir over low heat until smooth. Transfer to medium bowl; cool 10 minutes. Whisk in sifted flours, then whisk in egg.

4 Drop alternate spoonfuls of mixtures into pan holes. Pull skewer back and forth through cake mixture in each pan hole several times for a marbled effect. Bake about 30 minutes.

5 Meanwhile, make dark chocolate and white chocolate ganache.

6 Stand cakes in pans 5 minutes before turning, top-side up, onto wire racks to cool.

7 Spread cold cakes with dark chocolate ganache; dollop cakes with spoonfuls of white chocolate ganache. Using knife, swirl back and forth through ganache for marbled effect.

dark chocolate ganache Stir cream and chocolate in small saucepan over low heat until smooth. Cool 15 minutes or until spreadable.

white chocolate ganache Stir cream and chocolate in small saucepan over low heat until smooth. Cool 15 minutes or until spreadable.

GRADUATION CAKES

prep + cook time **1 hour (+ cooling)** makes **12**

dark chocolate mud cakes

60g (2 ounces) dark (semi-sweet) eating chocolate, chopped coarsely
⅔ cup (160ml) water
90g (3 ounces) butter, softened
1 cup (220g) firmly packed light brown sugar
2 eggs
⅔ cup (100g) self-raising flour
2 tablespoons cocoa powder
⅓ cup (40g) ground almonds

white chocolate ganache

½ cup (125ml) pouring cream
345g (11 ounces) white eating chocolate, chopped coarsely

decorations

12 Maltesers
12 thin dark (semi-sweet) chocolate squares
20cm (8-inch) piece black licorice strap
30g (1 ounce) dark (semi-sweet) eating chocolate, melted

1 Preheat oven to 170°C/340°F. Line 12-hole (⅓-cup/80ml) muffin pan with paper cases.

2 Stir chocolate and the water in small saucepan over low heat until smooth.

3 Beat butter, sugar and eggs in small bowl with electric mixer until light and fluffy. Stir in sifted flour and cocoa, ground almonds and warm chocolate mixture. Drop ¼ cups of mixture into paper cases.

4 Bake about 25 minutes. Stand cakes in pan 5 minutes before turning, top-side up, onto wire rack to cool.

5 Make white chocolate ganache. Spread cold cakes with ganache.

6 Place a Malteser in centre of each cake, position chocolate square on Malteser to make a mortarboard. Cut thin strips, about 4cm (1½ inches) long, from licorice strap; split the end of each strip into finer strips to make tassels. Attach a tassel to each mortarboard with a tiny dab of the melted chocolate.

white chocolate ganache Bring cream to the boil in small saucepan; remove from heat. When bubbles subside, add chocolate; stir until smooth. Cover; stand at room temperature 15 minutes or until ganache is spreadable.

TOFFEE TUMBLES

prep + cook time **3 hours 30 minutes (+ cooling)** makes **12**

almond butter cakes

155g (5 ounces) butter, softened
½ teaspoon almond extract
⅔ cup (150g) caster (superfine) sugar
2 eggs
⅓ cup (50g) self-raising flour
½ cup (75g) plain (all-purpose) flour
½ cup (60g) ground almonds

choux puffs

60g (2 ounces) butter
¾ cup (180ml) water
¾ cup (110g) plain (all-purpose) flour
3 eggs, beaten lightly

vanilla custard

1¼ cups (310ml) milk
1 vanilla bean, split
4 egg yolks
½ cup (110g) caster (superfine) sugar
¼ cup (40g) cornflour (cornstarch)

toffee

1 cup (220g) caster (superfine) sugar
½ cup (125ml) water

1 Make choux puffs; make vanilla custard.
2 Line 12-hole (⅓-cup/80ml) muffin pan with paper cases.
3 Beat butter, extract, sugar and eggs in small bowl with electric mixer until light and fluffy. Stir in sifted flours and ground almonds, in two batches. Divide mixture into paper cases; smooth surface.
4 Bake about 20 minutes at 180°C/350°F. Stand cakes in pan 5 minutes before turning, top-side up, onto wire rack to cool.
5 Cut 2cm (¾-inch) deep hole in centre of cold cakes, fill with custard; replace lid. Spread cakes with a little more custard; top with a layer of puffs. Stack remaining puffs on cakes, dipping each in a little custard to hold in place.
6 Make toffee; drizzle over puffs.

choux puffs Preheat oven to 220°C/425°F. Grease oven trays, line with baking paper. Combine butter and the water in medium saucepan; bring to the boil. Add flour; beat with a wooden spoon over heat until mixture forms a smooth ball. Transfer mixture to small bowl; beat in egg with electric mixer, in about six batches, until mixture becomes glossy. Spoon mixture into piping bag fitted with a 1cm (½-inch) plain tube. Pipe about 300 tiny dollops of pastry (about ¼ level teaspoon each), 2cm (¾ inch) apart, onto trays; bake 7 minutes. Reduce oven temperature to 180°C/350°F; bake puffs a further 5 minutes or until crisp (see tip). Leave oven on to bake cupcakes.

vanilla custard Boil milk and vanilla bean in small saucepan; remove from heat, discard bean. Beat egg yolks, sugar and cornflour in small bowl with electric mixer until thick. Gradually beat in warm milk; return to pan. Stir over heat until mixture boils and thickens. Cover surface of custard with plastic wrap; cool.

toffee Stir sugar and the water in small heavy-based saucepan over heat, without boiling, until sugar dissolves. Boil, then simmer, uncovered, without stirring, until mixture is golden. Remove from heat; stand until bubbles subside before using.

tip **If cooking in batches, choux puffs must be baked for the total cooking time before the next batch can be baked.**

CHOCOLATE VALENTINES

prep + cook time **1 hour 45 minutes** makes **12**

double chocolate raspberry cakes

60g (2 ounces) dark (semi-sweet) eating chocolate, chopped coarsely
½ cup (125ml) water
90g (3 ounces) butter, softened
1 cup (220g) firmly packed light brown sugar
2 eggs
⅔ cup (100g) self-raising flour
2 tablespoons cocoa powder
⅓ cup (40g) ground almonds
100g (3½ ounces) frozen raspberries

decorations

2 tablespoons cocoa powder
1kg (2 pounds) ready-made chocolate icing
8cm (3-inch) round cutter
⅓ cup (110g) raspberry jam, warmed, strained
½ cup (80g) icing (confectioners') sugar
155g (5 ounces) ready-made red icing
155g (5 ounces) ready-made white icing
pink food colouring
5cm, 4.5cm and 3cm (2-inch, 1.5-inch and 1-inch) heart-shaped cutters

1 Preheat oven to 170°C/340°F. Line 12-hole (⅓-cup/80ml) muffin pan with paper cases.
2 Combine chopped chocolate and the water in small saucepan; stir over low heat until smooth.
3 Beat butter, sugar and eggs in small bowl with electric mixer until just combined. Stir in sifted flour and cocoa, ground almonds, then the warm chocolate mixture; gently fold in raspberries. Divide mixture into paper cases; smooth surface.
4 Bake about 45 minutes. Stand cakes in pan 5 minutes before turning, top-side up, onto wire rack to cool. Remove paper cases from cold cakes.
5 Dust work surface with sifted cocoa, knead chocolate icing until smooth. Roll out until 5mm (¼ inch) thick. Using cutter, cut 8cm (3-inch) rounds from icing. Brush cakes with jam; cover cakes with chocolate rounds.
6 Dust work surface with sifted icing sugar, knead red and white icing, separately, until smooth. Use food colouring to tint 100g (3½ ounces) of the white icing pink and remaining white icing a paler pink.
7 Roll each coloured icing to a thickness of 5mm (¼ inch). Using heart-shaped cutters, cut out hearts from icings using picture as a guide.
8 Decorate cakes with hearts; brush each with a little water to secure to the other.

tip **This recipe also makes 6 texas muffins (¾-cup/180ml); bake about 55 minutes.**

HUGS & KISSES

prep + cook time **1 hour** makes **12**

marble cakes

125g (4 ounces) butter, softened
1 teaspoon vanilla extract
⅔ cup (150g) caster (superfine) sugar
2 eggs
1¼ cups (185g) self-raising flour
⅓ cup (80ml) milk
pink food colouring
1 tablespoon cocoa powder
2 teaspoons milk, extra

butter cream

125g (4 ounces) butter, softened
1½ cups (240g) icing (confectioners') sugar
2 tablespoons milk
pink food colouring

decorations

white sugar heart-shaped lollies

1 Preheat oven to 180°C/350°F. Line 12-hole (⅓-cup/80ml) muffin pan with paper cases.
2 Beat butter, extract, sugar and eggs in small bowl with electric mixer until fluffy. Stir in sifted flour and milk, in two batches.
3 Divide mixture among three small bowls. Tint one mixture pink. Blend sifted cocoa with extra milk in cup; stir into the second bowl of mixture. Leave the third bowl of mixture plain.
4 Drop alternate spoonfuls of mixtures into paper cases. Pull a skewer through mixtures for a marbled effect.
5 Bake about 20 minutes. Stand cakes in pan 5 minutes before turning, top-side up, onto wire rack to cool.
6 Make butter cream. Spread cold cakes with butter cream. Position heart-shaped lollies on cakes – in a cross for kisses and a circle for hugs.
butter cream Beat butter in small bowl with electric mixer until as white as possible; beat in sifted icing sugar and milk, in two batches. Tint butter cream pink with food colouring.

PINEAPPLE HIBISCUS CAKES

prep + cook time **2 hours (+ drying)** makes **12**

pineapple carrot cakes

½ cup (125ml) vegetable oil
3 eggs, beaten lightly
1½ cups (225g) self-raising flour
¾ cup (165g) caster (superfine) sugar
½ teaspoon ground cinnamon
2 cups firmly packed coarsely grated carrot
¾ cup (160g) drained crushed pineapple

pineapple flowers

1 tablespoon caster (superfine) sugar
1 tablespoon water
12 wafer thin slices fresh pineapple

lemon cream cheese frosting

30g (1 ounce) butter, softened
90g (3 ounces) cream cheese, softened
1 teaspoon finely grated lemon rind
1½ cups (240g) icing (confectioners') sugar

1 Make pineapple flowers.
2 Increase oven temperature to 180°C/350°F. Line 12-hole (⅓-cup/80ml) muffin pan with paper cases.
3 Combine oil, eggs, sifted flour, sugar and cinnamon in medium bowl; stir until combined. Stir in carrot and pineapple. Divide mixture into paper cases.
4 Bake about 30 minutes. Stand cakes in pan 5 minutes before turning, top-side up, onto wire rack to cool.
5 Make lemon cream cheese frosting; spread over cold cakes. Top cakes with pineapple flowers.

pineapple flowers Preheat oven to 120°C/250°F. Stir sugar and the water in small saucepan over low heat until sugar has dissolved. Bring to the boil; boil 1 minute. Brush both sides of pineapple slices with sugar syrup. Place slices, in a single layer, on wire racks over oven trays. Dry pineapple in oven about 1 hour. Immediately remove slices from rack; carefully shape into flowers. Dry over an egg carton to maintain shape.

lemon cream cheese frosting Beat butter, cream cheese and rind in small bowl with electric mixer until light and fluffy; gradually beat in sifted icing sugar.

tip **This recipe also makes 6 texas muffins (¾-cup/180ml); bake about 40 minutes.**

TURKISH DELIGHTS

prep + cook time **55 minutes** makes **6**

white chocolate pistachio cakes

60g (2 ounces) white eating chocolate, chopped coarsely
2 tablespoons rosewater
½ cup (125ml) water
⅓ cup (45g) roasted unsalted shelled pistachios
90g (3 ounces) butter, softened
1 cup (220g) firmly packed light brown sugar
2 eggs
⅔ cup (100g) self-raising flour
2 tablespoons plain (all-purpose) flour

decorations

⅔ cup (90g) roasted unsalted shelled pistachios
150g (5½ ounces) white eating chocolate, melted
900g (1¾ pounds) turkish delight, chopped coarsely

1 Preheat oven to 180°C/350°F. Line 6-hole texas muffin pan (¾-cup/180ml) with paper cases.

2 Combine chocolate, rosewater and the water in small saucepan; stir over low heat until smooth.

3 Blend or process nuts until fine.

4 Beat butter, sugar and eggs in small bowl with electric mixer until combined. Fold in sifted flours, ground nuts and warm chocolate mixture. Divide mixture into paper cases.

5 Bake about 35 minutes. Stand cakes in pan 5 minutes before turning, top-side up, onto wire rack to cool.

6 Cut a 2.5cm (1-inch) deep hole in the centre of each cold cake; fill with a few nuts, then drizzle with a little chocolate and replace lids.

7 Decorate cakes with pieces of turkish delight and remaining nuts, dipped in chocolate to secure.

tip **This recipe also makes 12 standard muffins (⅓-cup/80ml); bake about 25 minutes.**

SUGAR AND LACE

prep + cook time **50 minutes (+ cooling)** makes **12**

caramel mud cakes

125g (4 ounces) butter, chopped coarsely
100g (3½ ounces) white eating chocolate, chopped coarsely
⅔ cup (150g) firmly packed light brown sugar
¼ cup (90g) golden syrup (or treacle)
⅔ cup (160ml) milk
1 cup (150g) plain (all-purpose) flour
⅓ cup (50g) self-raising flour
1 egg

decorations

doily, lace or stencil
½ cup (80g) icing (confectioners') sugar

1 Preheat oven to 170°C/340°F. Line 12-hole (⅓-cup/80ml) muffin pan with paper cases.
2 Combine butter, chocolate, sugar, syrup and milk in small saucepan; stir over low heat until smooth. Transfer mixture to medium bowl; cool 15 minutes.
3 Whisk sifted flours into chocolate mixture, then whisk in egg. Divide mixture into paper cases.
4 Bake about 30 minutes. Stand cakes in pan 5 minutes before turning, top-side up, onto wire rack to cool.
5 Place doily, lace or stencil over cold cake; sift a little icing sugar over doily, then carefully lift doily from cake. Repeat with remaining cakes and icing sugar.

tip **This recipe also makes 6 texas muffins (¾-cup/180ml); bake about 40 minutes.**

TOFFEE APPLE TOWERS

prep + cook time **1 hour (+ standing)** makes **12**

maple, pecan and apple cakes

60g (2 ounces) butter, softened
1 cup (150g) self-raising flour
1 teaspoon ground cinnamon
½ cup (110g) firmly packed light brown sugar
¼ cup (60ml) pure maple syrup
2 eggs
⅔ cup (80g) coarsely chopped pecans
½ cup (85g) coarsely grated apple

maple frosting

90g (3 ounces) butter, softened
1 cup (160g) icing (confectioners') sugar
2 teaspoons pure maple syrup

toffee

1 cup (220g) caster (superfine) sugar
½ cup (125ml) water

1 Preheat oven to 180°C/350°F. Line 12-hole (⅓-cup/80ml) muffin pan with paper cases.
2 Beat butter, sifted flour and cinnamon, sugar, syrup and eggs in small bowl with electric mixer on low speed until ingredients are combined. Increase speed to medium; beat until mixture has changed to a paler colour. Stir in nuts and grated apple. Divide mixture into paper cases; smooth surface.
3 Bake about 25 minutes. Stand cakes in pan 5 minutes before turning, top-side up, onto wire rack to cool.
4 Make maple frosting. Make toffee.
5 Spread cold cakes with frosting; decorate with toffee shards.

maple frosting Beat butter, sifted icing sugar and syrup in small bowl with electric mixer until light and fluffy.

toffee Stir sugar and the water in small saucepan over heat, without boiling, until sugar has dissolved; bring to the boil. Reduce heat; simmer, uncovered, without stirring, until mixture is golden brown. Remove from heat; stand until bubbles subside. To make toffee shards, drizzle toffee over baking-paper-lined oven tray. Stand at room temperature until set.

tip **This recipe also makes 6 texas muffins (¾-cup/180ml); bake about 35 minutes.**

WHITE CHOCOLATE CURLS

prep + cook time **1 hour (+ cooling & standing)** makes **12**

white chocolate mud cakes

125g (4 ounces) butter, chopped coarsely
75g (2½ ounces) white eating chocolate, chopped coarsely
1 cup (220g) caster (superfine) sugar
½ cup (125ml) milk
½ cup (75g) plain (all-purpose) flour
½ cup (75g) self-raising flour
1 egg

white chocolate ganache

½ cup (125ml) pouring cream
345g (11 ounces) white eating chocolate, chopped coarsely

decorations

185g (6 ounces) white eating chocolate

1 Preheat oven to 170°C/340°F. Line 12-hole (⅓-cup/80ml) muffin pan with paper cases.
2 Stir butter, chocolate, sugar and milk in small saucepan over low heat until smooth. Transfer mixture to medium bowl; cool 15 minutes.
3 Whisk sifted flours into chocolate mixture, then whisk in egg. Drop ¼ cups of mixture into paper cases.
4 Bake about 30 minutes. Stand cakes in pan 5 minutes before turning, top-side up, onto wire rack to cool.
5 Make white chocolate ganache. Spread cold cakes with ganache.
6 Run vegetable peeler down side of chocolate to make curls; top cakes with chocolate curls.
white chocolate ganache Bring cream to the boil in small saucepan; remove from heat. When bubbles subside, add chocolate; stir until smooth. Cover; stand at room temperature 15 minutes or until ganache is spreadable.

SWEET GINGER ACES

prep + cook time **1 hour 30 minutes** makes **6**

ginger buttermilk cakes

½ cup (110g) firmly packed light brown sugar
½ cup (75g) plain (all-purpose) flour
½ cup (75g) self-raising flour
¼ teaspoon bicarbonate of soda (baking soda)
1 teaspoon ground ginger
½ teaspoon ground cinnamon
¼ teaspoon ground nutmeg
90g (3 ounces) butter, softened
1 egg
¼ cup (60ml) buttermilk
2 tablespoons golden syrup (or treacle)

decorations

½ cup (80g) icing (confectioners') sugar
400g (12½ ounces) ready-made white icing
⅓ cup (110g) ginger marmalade, warmed, strained
9cm (3¾-inch) round cutter
50g (1½ ounces) ready-made red icing
50g (1½ ounces) ready-made black icing
heart, diamond, club and spade cutters
'A' alphabet cutter

1 Preheat oven to 170°C/340°F. Line 6-hole (¾-cup/180ml) texas muffin pan with paper cases.

2 Sift dry ingredients into small bowl, then add remaining ingredients. Beat mixture with electric mixer on low speed until ingredients are combined. Increase speed to medium; beat until mixture is changed to a paler colour. Divide mixture into paper cases; smooth surface.

3 Bake about 40 minutes. Stand cakes in pan 5 minutes before turning, top-side up, onto wire rack to cool.

4 Dust work surface with sifted icing sugar; knead white icing until smooth. Brush cold cakes with marmalade. Roll icing out to 5mm (¼-inch) thickness. Using 9cm (3¾-inch) round cutter, cut 6 rounds from icing. Place rounds on cakes; tie cakes with ribbon.

5 Roll red and black icing out, separately, to 5mm (¼-inch) thickness. Cut out shapes using heart, diamond, club and spade cutters.

6 Roll out red and black icing scraps, separately, to 2mm (⅛-inch) thickness. Cut out 'A's using alphabet cutter.

7 Secure icing shapes to cakes by brushing backs with a tiny amount of water.

tip **This recipe also makes 12 standard muffins (⅓-cup/80ml); bake about 30 minutes. Use an 8cm (3¼-inch) round cutter for smaller cakes.**

COCONUT KISSES

prep + cook time **1 hour (+ refrigeration)** makes **12**

white chocolate mud cakes

125g (4 ounces) butter, chopped coarsely
80g (2½ ounces) white eating chocolate, chopped coarsely
1 cup (220g) caster (superfine) sugar
½ cup (125ml) milk
½ cup (75g) plain (all-purpose) flour
½ cup (75g) self-raising flour
½ teaspoon coconut extract
1 egg

whipped white chocolate ganache

¼ cup (60ml) pouring cream
185g (6 ounces) white eating chocolate, chopped coarsely
1 tablespoon coconut-flavoured liqueur

decorations

450g (14½ ounces) ferrero raffaelo chocolate truffles

1 Preheat oven to 170°C/340°F. Line 12-hole (⅓-cup/80ml) muffin pan with paper cases.
2 Combine butter, chocolate, sugar and milk in small saucepan; stir over low heat until smooth. Transfer mixture to medium bowl; cool 15 minutes.
3 Whisk in sifted flours, then extract and egg. Divide mixture into paper cases; smooth surface.
4 Bake about 30 minutes. Stand cakes in pan 5 minutes before turning, top-side up, onto wire rack to cool.
5 Make whipped white chocolate ganache.
6 Spread cakes with ganache. Top with halved truffles, then stack with whole truffles using a little ganache to secure.

whipped white chocolate ganache Bring cream to the boil in small saucepan; remove from heat. When bubbles subside, add chocolate and liqueur; stir until smooth. Transfer mixture to small bowl. Cover; refrigerate 30 minutes. Beat with an electric mixer until light and fluffy.

tip **This recipe also makes 6 texas muffins (¾-cup/180ml); bake about 40 minutes.**

KALEIDOCAKES

prep + cook time **1 hour 30 minutes** makes **12**

orange butter cakes

90g (3 ounces) butter, softened
90g (3 ounces) cream cheese, softened
2 teaspoons finely grated orange rind
⅔ cup (150g) caster (superfine) sugar
2 eggs
⅓ cup (50g) self-raising flour
½ cup (75g) plain (all-purpose) flour

white icing

300g (9½ ounces) ready-made white icing, chopped coarsely
1 egg white
¼ teaspoon orange extract

royal icing

1½ cups (240g) pure icing (confectioners') sugar
1 egg white
½ teaspoon lemon juice
yellow, orange, green, pink and purple food colouring

1 Preheat oven to 180°C/350°F. Line 12-hole (⅓-cup/80ml) muffin pan with paper cases.
2 Beat butter, cheese, rind, sugar and eggs in small bowl with electric mixer until light and fluffy. Beat in flours on low speed until combined. Divide mixture into paper cases; smooth surface.
3 Bake about 20 minutes. Stand cakes in pan 5 minutes before turning, top-side up, onto wire rack to cool.
4 Make white icing. Spread icing quickly over cakes; use a metal spatula dipped in hot water to smooth surface. Stand at room temperature until set.
5 Make royal icing. Divide evenly between five small bowls. Using colourings, tint icing yellow, orange, green, pink and purple; cover each tightly with plastic wrap when you are not using them. Spoon coloured icings, separately, into small disposable piping bags; pipe patterns onto cakes using picture as a guide.
white icing Place icing in small heatproof bowl over small saucepan of simmering water; stir until smooth. Stir in egg white and extract. Stand at room temperature about 10 minutes, or until thickened slightly.
royal icing Sift icing sugar through very fine sieve. Lightly beat egg white in small bowl with electric mixer; add icing sugar, a tablespoon at a time. When icing reaches firm peaks, use a wooden spoon to beat in juice; cover tightly with plastic wrap.

tip **This recipe also makes 6 texas muffins (¾-cup/180ml); bake about 30 minutes.**

COCONUT CHERRY HEARTS

prep + cook time **1 hour 30 minutes (+ standing)** makes **12**

choc-chip cherry cakes

125g (4 ounces) butter, softened
½ teaspoon coconut extract
⅔ cup (150g) caster (superfine) sugar
2 eggs
⅓ cup (80ml) milk
½ cup (40g) desiccated coconut
⅓ cup (70g) red glacé cherries, chopped coarsely
50g (1½ ounces) dark eating (semi-sweet) chocolate, chopped coarsely
1 cup (150g) self-raising flour
¼ cup (35g) plain (all-purpose) flour

milk chocolate ganache

¼ cup (60ml) pouring cream
100g (3 ounces) milk eating chocolate, chopped coarsely

decorations

150g (4½ ounces) white chocolate Melts, melted
pink food colouring

1 Preheat oven to 180°C/350°F. Line 12-hole (⅓-cup/80ml) muffin pan with paper cases.

2 Beat butter, extract, sugar and eggs in small bowl with electric mixer until combined. Stir in milk, coconut, cherries and chocolate, then sifted flours. Divide mixture into paper cases; smooth surface.

3 Bake about 25 minutes. Stand cakes in pan 5 minutes before turning, top-side up, onto wire rack to cool.

4 Make milk chocolate ganache.

5 Divide melted white chocolate evenly between three small bowls; tint two portions with two different shades of pink. Spoon coloured chocolate mixtures, separately, into small disposable piping bags; pipe different coloured heart shapes in varying sizes, onto baking-paper-lined tray. Stand at room temperature until set.

6 Spread cakes with ganache; decorate with coloured hearts.

milk chocolate ganache Bring cream to the boil in small saucepan; remove from heat. When bubbles subside, add chocolate; stir until smooth. Cover; stand at room temperature 15 minutes or until ganache is spreadable.

tip **This recipe also makes 6 texas muffins (¾-cup/180ml); bake about 35 minutes.**

CITRUS CAKES

prep + cook time **2 hours (+ standing)** makes **12**

poppy seed citrus cakes

¼ cup (40g) poppy seeds
2 tablespoons milk
125g (4 ounces) butter, softened
1 teaspoon finely grated lemon rind
1 teaspoon finely grated lime rind
⅔ cup (150g) caster (superfine) sugar
2 eggs
1 cup (150g) self-raising flour
⅓ cup (50g) plain (all-purpose) flour
⅓ cup (40g) ground almonds
¼ cup (60ml) orange juice

decorations

½ cup (80g) icing (confectioners') sugar
450g (14½ ounces) ready-made white icing
green, orange and yellow food colouring
⅓ cup (110g) orange marmalade, warmed, strained
8cm (3¼-inch) round cutter
2 tablespoons green sprinkles
2 tablespoons orange sprinkles
2 tablespoons yellow sprinkles

1 Preheat oven to 180°C/350°F. Line 12-hole (⅓-cup/80ml) muffin pan with paper cases.
2 Combine seeds and milk in small bowl; stand 20 minutes.
3 Beat butter, rinds, sugar and eggs in small bowl with electric mixer until light and fluffy. Stir in sifted flours, ground almonds, juice and poppy seed mixture. Divide mixture into paper cases; smooth surface.
4 Bake about 20 minutes. Stand cakes in pan 5 minutes before turning, top-side up, onto wire rack to cool.
5 Dust work surface with sifted icing sugar; knead ready-made icing until smooth. Reserve 100g (3 ounces) of icing; enclose in plastic wrap. Divide remaining icing into three equal portions; knead green, orange and yellow colouring into icings. Enclose separately in plastic wrap.
6 Brush cold cakes with marmalade. Roll each of the coloured portions of icing out to 5mm (¼-inch) thickness. Using round cutter, cut 12 rounds from icing. Place rounds on cakes.
7 Roll reserved white icing into very thin lengths, cut off small pieces for seeds. Position lengths on top of cakes, using a little water to secure, for segments.
8 Fill segments with matching coloured sprinkles; position icing seeds.

tips **This recipe also makes 6 texas muffins (¾-cup/180ml); bake about 30 minutes. We used green, orange and yellow paper muffin cases to match the decorations of these lovely cakes.**

DRAGONFLY

prep + cook time **1 hour** makes **15**

quick-mix chocolate cakes
1 cup (150g) self-raising flour
½ cup (75g) plain (all-purpose) flour
⅓ cup (35g) cocoa powder
¾ cup (165g) caster (superfine) sugar
185g (6 ounces) butter, softened
3 eggs
½ cup (125ml) milk
chocolate butter cream
125g (4 ounces) butter, softened
1½ cups (240g) icing (confectioners') sugar
2 tablespoons cocoa powder
2 tablespoons milk
decorations
60 white Choc Bits
4 big speckles (5.5cm/2¼ inches)
2 tablespoons shredded coconut

1 Preheat oven to 180°C/350°F. Line 15 holes of two 12-hole (⅓-cup/80ml) muffin pans with paper cases.
2 Sift dry ingredients into medium bowl, add remaining ingredients; beat with electric mixer on low speed until combined. Increase speed to medium; beat until mixture is smooth and changed to a paler colour. Drop ¼ cups of mixture into paper cases.
3 Bake about 20 minutes. Stand cakes in pans 5 minutes before turning, top-side up, onto wire racks to cool.
4 Make chocolate butter cream.
5 Spread the tops of cakes with a thick layer of butter cream. Make the dragonfly bodies using four white Choc Bits each. Cut big speckles into quarters, position two quarters on each cake for wings. Position coconut for antennae.
chocolate butter cream Beat butter in small bowl with electric mixer until as white as possible; beat in sifted icing sugar and cocoa, and milk, in two batches.

EXTRAIT

HIGH HEELS

prep + cook time **1 hour 20 minutes (+ standing)** makes **12**

dark chocolate mud cakes

60g (2 ounces) dark (semi-sweet) eating chocolate, chopped coarsely
⅔ cup (160ml) water
90g (3 ounces) butter, softened
1 cup (220g) firmly packed light brown sugar
2 eggs
⅔ cup (100g) self-raising flour
2 tablespoons cocoa powder
⅓ cup (40g) ground almonds

white chocolate ganache

½ cup (125ml) pouring cream
345g (11 ounces) white eating chocolate, chopped coarsely

decorations

12 small pink edible sugar butterflies
12 chocolate high-heeled shoes

1 Preheat oven to 170°C/340°F. Line 12-hole (⅓-cup/80ml) muffin pan with paper cases.
2 Stir chocolate and the water in small saucepan over low heat until smooth.
3 Beat butter, sugar and eggs in small bowl with electric mixer until light and fluffy. Stir in sifted flour and cocoa, ground almonds and warm chocolate mixture. Drop ¼ cups of mixture into paper cases.
4 Bake about 25 minutes. Stand cakes in pan 5 minutes before turning, top-side up, onto wire rack to cool.
5 Make white chocolate ganache. Spread cold cakes with ganache.
6 Attach sugar butterflies to chocolate shoes with tiny dabs of ganache. Position shoes on cakes.

white chocolate ganache Bring cream to the boil in small saucepan; remove from heat. When bubbles subside, add chocolate; stir until smooth. Cover; stand at room temperature 15 minutes or until ganache is spreadable.

tip **Chocolate high-heeled shoes are available from specialty cake-decorating stores.**

CHOCKY LIPS

prep + cook time **1 hour 20 minutes (+ standing)** makes **9**

flourless choc-hazelnut cakes

¼ cup (25g) cocoa powder
¼ cup (60ml) hot water
100g (3½ ounces) dark (semi-sweet) eating chocolate, melted
100g (3½ ounces) butter, melted
1 cup (220g) firmly packed light brown sugar
¾ cup (75g) ground hazelnuts
3 eggs, separated

dark chocolate ganache

½ cup (125ml) pouring cream
200g (6½ ounces) dark (semi-sweet) eating chocolate, chopped coarsely

decorations

red cake sparkles
9 red lolly lips

1 Preheat oven to 180°C/350°F. Line nine holes of 12-hole (⅓-cup/80ml) muffin pan with paper cases.
2 Blend cocoa with the water in medium bowl until smooth. Stir in chocolate, butter, sugar, nuts and egg yolks.
3 Beat egg whites in small bowl with electric mixer until soft peaks form; fold into chocolate mixture, in two batches. Pour ⅓ cups of mixture into paper cases.
4 Bake about 25 minutes. Stand cakes in pan 5 minutes before turning, top-side up, onto wire rack to cool.
5 Make dark chocolate ganache.
6 Dollop a generous amount of ganache on top of each cold cake. Sprinkle with cake sparkles; top with lolly lips.

dark chocolate ganache Bring cream to the boil in small saucepan; remove from heat. When bubbles subside, add chocolate; stir until smooth. Cover; stand at room temperature 30 minutes or until thick and spreadable.

ALMONDS

extract *see* essence/extract.

ground also known as almond meal; nuts powdered to a coarse flour-like texture.

BAKING POWDER a raising agent consisting mainly of two parts cream of tartar to one part bicarbonate of soda (baking soda). The acid and alkaline combination, when moistened and heated, gives off carbon dioxide which aerates and lightens a mixture during baking.

BICARBONATE OF SODA (BAKING SODA) also known as bicarb soda; a mild alkali used as a leavening agent in baking.

BUTTER use salted or unsalted (sweet) butter; 125g is equal to one stick (4 ounces) of butter.

BUTTERMILK originally the term given to the slightly sour liquid left after butter was churned from cream, today it is made similarly to yogurt. Sold alongside fresh milk in supermarkets. Despite the implication of its name, it is low in fat.

CACHOUS also called dragées in some countries; minuscule (3mm to 5mm) metallic-looking-but-edible confectionery balls used in cake decorating; available in silver, gold or various colours.

CARAMEL TOP 'N' FILL a caramel filling made from milk and cane sugar. Can be used straight from the can for cheesecakes, slices, tarts and pies. A similar quality to sweetened condensed milk, only a thicker, caramel consistency.

CAROB seed of a Mediterranean tree which can be used as a substitute for chocolate; can be purchased in health food stores.

CHERRIES

glacé also called candied cherries; boiled in sugar syrup, then dried.

maraschino cherries that have been soaked, flavoured and often coloured, resulting in a sweet, bright, glossy fruit, perfect for garnish. They can be bought in jars at most supermarkets, greengrocers and specialty food shops.

CHOCOLATE

Choc Bits also known as chocolate chips or chocolate morsels; come in milk, white and dark chocolate varieties. Contain an emulsifier, so hold their shape in baking and are ideal for decorating.

dark eating (semi-sweet) also known as luxury chocolate; made of a high percentage of cocoa liquor and cocoa butter, and a little added sugar.

Melts small discs of compound milk, white or dark chocolate ideal for melting and moulding.

milk eating the most popular eating chocolate, mild and very sweet; similar in make-up to dark eating chocolate, with the difference being the addition of milk solids.

white eating contains no cocoa solids but derives its sweet flavour from cocoa butter. It is very sensitive to heat, so watch carefully if melting.

CINNAMON available both in the piece (called sticks or quills) and ground into powder; one of the world's most common spices, used for both sweet and savoury foods.

COCOA POWDER also known as unsweetened cocoa; cocoa beans (cacao seeds) that have been fermented, roasted, shelled, ground into powder then cleared of most of the fat content.

COCONUT

desiccated dried, unsweetened, finely shredded coconut.

extract *see* essence/extract.

flaked dried, flaked coconut flesh.

flavoured liqueur we use Malibu; you can use your favourite brand.

freshly grated can be grated from a whole fresh coconut or purchased, frozen, in packets.

shredded dried coconut strips.

COFFEE LIQUEUR we use Kahlúa or Tia Maria, but you can use your favourite brand.

CORNFLOUR (CORNSTARCH) used as a thickening agent. Available as 100% maize (corn) and wheaten cornflour.

CREAM

pouring also known as pure cream and fresh cream; has no additives unlike commercially thickened cream. Minimum fat content 35%.

sour thick commercially-cultured soured cream. Minimum fat content 35%.

thick we used thick cream with 48% fat content.

thickened (heavy) a whipping cream containing a thickener. Minimum fat content 35%.

CREAM CHEESE also known as Philadelphia or Philly, a soft cows'-milk cheese.

light cream cheese a spreadable blend of cottage and cream cheeses. Sold in supermarkets.

CURRANTS, DRIED tiny, almost black raisins so-named after a grape variety that originated in Corinth, Greece.

CUSTARD POWDER instant mixture used to make pouring custard, similar to instant pudding mixes.

GLOSSARY

EGGS we use large chicken eggs with an average weight of 60g. Store eggs, in the carton they come in, under refrigeration as soon as you bring them home to slow down deterioration. This helps reduce water loss and protects them from absorbing flavour from other fridge items. Most eggs can be kept, in their carton, in the fridge, for up to 4 weeks. If a recipe calls for raw or barely cooked eggs; exercise caution if there is a salmonella problem in your community, particularly in food eaten by children and pregnant women.

ESSENCE/EXTRACT an essence is either a distilled concentration of a food quality or an artificial creation of it. Coconut and almond essences are synthetically produced substances used in small amounts to impart their respective flavours to foods. An extract is made by actually extracting the flavour from a food product. In the case of vanilla, pods are soaked, usually in alcohol, to capture the authentic flavour. Both extracts and essences will keep indefinitely if stored in a cool dark place.

FLAKE a small chocolate bar consisting of layers of "flaky" chocolate, hence the name.

FLOUR

plain (all-purpose) flour made from wheat.

self-raising plain flour sifted with baking powder in the proportion of 1 cup flour to 2 teaspoons baking powder.

GELATINE we use dried (powdered) gelatine in this book; it's also available in sheet form known as leaf gelatine.

GINGER

fresh also called green or root ginger; the thick gnarled root of a tropical plant. Can be kept, peeled, covered with dry sherry in a jar and refrigerated, or frozen in an airtight container.

glacé fresh ginger root preserved in sugar syrup; crystallised ginger (sweetened with cane sugar) can be substituted if rinsed with warm water and dried before using.

ground also called powdered ginger; used as a flavouring in baking but cannot be substituted for fresh ginger.

GOLDEN SYRUP a by-product of refined sugarcane; pure maple syrup or honey can be substituted.

HAZELNUTS also known as filberts; plump, grape-sized, rich, sweet nut.

meal known as ground hazelnuts.

HUNDREDS & THOUSANDS nonpareils; tiny sugar-syrup-coated sugar crystals that come in many bright colours. Used to decorate cakes and party foods.

JAFFA ball-shaped confectionary with a smooth chocolate centre and an orange-flavoured crisp shell.

JAM also known as preserve or conserve; usually made from fruit.

JELLY CRYSTALS a powdered mixture of gelatine, sweetener, and artificial fruit flavouring that's used to make a moulded, translucent, quivering dessert. Also known as jello.

LEMON BUTTER also known as lemon cheese or lemon spread; a smooth spread, usually made from lemons, butter and eggs.

LICORICE an aniseed-flavoured confection which comes in straps, tubes and twisted ropes.

LOLLIES confectionery; also known as sweets or candy.

MALTESERS chocolates with crisp, light honeycomb centres; made from chocolate, glucose syrup, malt extract, milk powder, flour and sugar.

MAPLE-FLAVOURED SYRUP is made from sugar cane and is also known as golden or pancake syrup. It is not a substitute for pure maple syrup.

MAPLE SYRUP, PURE distilled from the sap of sugar maple trees. Most often eaten with pancakes or waffles, but also used as an ingredient in baking or in preparing desserts. Maple-flavoured syrup or pancake syrup is not an adequate substitute for the real thing.

MARMALADE a preserve, usually based on citrus fruit and its rind, cooked with sugar until the mixture has an intense flavour and thick consistency. Orange, lemon and lime are some of the commercially prepared varieties available.

MARSHMALLOWS pink and white; made from sugar, glucose, gelatine and cornflour.

MILK we use full-cream homogenised milk unless otherwise specified.

sweetened condensed a canned milk product consisting of milk with more than half the water content removed and sugar added to the remaining milk.

MIXED DRIED FRUIT a mix of sultanas, raisins, mixed peel, currants and cherries.

MIXED PEEL candied citrus peel.

MIXED SPICE a blend of ground spices usually consisting of cinnamon, allspice and nutmeg.

NUTMEG a strong and pungent spice ground from the dried nut of an evergreen tree native to Indonesia. Usually ground but the flavour is more intense from a whole nut, available from spice shops, so it's best to grate your own. Used most often in baking and milk-based desserts, but also works nicely in savoury dishes.

NUTS, HOW TO ROAST place shelled, peeled nuts, in a single layer, on an oven tray, roast in a moderate oven for 8-10 minutes. Take care to avoid burning nuts.

OIL

cooking spray we use a cholesterol-free cooking spray made from canola oil.

olive made from ripened olives. Extra virgin and virgin are the first and second press, respectively, of the olives and are therefore considered the best; the "extra light" or "light" name on other types refers to taste not fat levels.

vegetable any of a number of oils sourced from plant rather than animal fats.

ORANGE EXTRACT *see* essence/extract.

PECANS native to the US and now grown locally; pecans are golden brown, buttery and rich. Good in savoury as well as sweet dishes; walnuts are a good substitute.

PEPPERMINT EXTRACT *see* essence/extract.

POPPY SEEDS tiny black seeds with a pungent flavour; store in an airtight container in a cool place or freezer.

READY-MADE ICING also called soft icing, ready-to-roll and prepared fondant.

RHUBARB only eat its thick, celery-like stalks, as the leaves contain a toxic substance.

ROSEWATER distilled from rose petals and used in the Middle East, North Africa, and India to flavour desserts. Don't confuse rosewater with rose essence, which is a more concentrated form.

SEMOLINA made from durum wheat; milled into either fine or coarse granules.

SUGAR

brown, light soft, finely granulated sugar retaining molasses for its characteristic colour and flavour.

caster (superfine) also known as finely granulated table sugar.

cinnamon combination of ground cinnamon and caster sugar.

demerara a rich, golden-coloured small-grained crystal sugar with a subtle molasses flavour.

icing (confectioners') also known as powdered sugar; granulated sugar crushed together with a small amount of added cornflour.

icing (confectioners'), pure also known as confectioners' or powdered sugar; granulated sugar crushed without the addition of cornflour.

palm also known as *nam tan pip*, *jaggery*, *jawa* or *gula melaka*; made from the sap of the sugar palm tree. Light brown to black in colour and usually sold in rock-hard cakes; substitute with brown sugar if unavailable.

raw natural, light-brown coloured coarsely granulated sugar.

white a coarse, granulated table sugar; also known as crystal sugar.

SULTANAS dried grapes; also known as golden raisins.

TREACLE thick, dark syrup not unlike molasses; a by-product of sugar refining.

VANILLA

bean dried long, thin pod from a tropical golden orchid; the minuscule black seeds inside the bean are used to impart a luscious vanilla flavour in baking and desserts. A whole bean can be placed in the sugar container to make the vanilla sugar often called for in sweet recipes.

extract *see* essence/extract. Only a couple of drops are needed to flavour most dishes. Imitation vanilla extract/essence is not a satisfactory substitute.

paste made from vanilla pods and contains real seeds. It is highly concentrated — one teaspoon replaces a whole vanilla pod without mess or fuss, as you neither have to split or scrape the pod. It is found in the baking aisle of supermarkets.

VIOLET CRUMBLE a honeycomb bar coated in milk chocolate.

VODKA distilled from a fermented grain mash, which is distilled to remove all flavour. Made mainly from grain, the most common being corn, rye, and wheat, and occasionally from potatoes.

WALNUTS as well as being a good source of fibre and healthy oils, walnuts contain a range of vitamins, minerals and other plant components called phytochemicals. Walnuts are high in beneficial omega-3 fatty acids. Delicious in both sweet and savoury dishes, as well as baking, shelled walnuts are best stored, tightly covered, in the refrigerator.

YOGURT we use unflavoured plain yogurt unless specified.

CONVERSION CHART

MEASURES

One Australian metric measuring cup holds approximately 250ml, one Australian metric tablespoon holds 20ml, one Australian metric teaspoon holds 5ml.

The difference between one country's measuring cups and another's is within a 2- or 3-teaspoon variance, and will not affect your cooking results. North America, New Zealand and the United Kingdom use a 15ml tablespoon. All cup and spoon measurements are level. The most accurate way of measuring dry ingredients is to weigh them. When measuring liquids, use a clear glass or plastic jug with metric markings.

We use large eggs with an average weight of 60g.

DRY MEASURES

METRIC	IMPERIAL
15g	½oz
30g	1oz
60g	2oz
90g	3oz
125g	4oz (¼lb)
155g	5oz
185g	6oz
220g	7oz
250g	8oz (½lb)
280g	9oz
315g	10oz
345g	11oz
375g	12oz (¾lb)
410g	13oz
440g	14oz
470g	15oz
500g	16oz (1lb)
750g	24oz (1½lb)
1kg	32oz (2lb)

LIQUID MEASURES

METRIC	IMPERIAL
30ml	1 fluid oz
60ml	2 fluid oz
100ml	3 fluid oz
125ml	4 fluid oz
150ml	5 fluid oz
190ml	6 fluid oz
250ml	8 fluid oz
300ml	10 fluid oz
500ml	16 fluid oz
600ml	20 fluid oz
1000ml (1 litre)	1¾ pints

LENGTH MEASURES

METRIC	IMPERIAL
3mm	⅛in
6mm	¼in
1cm	½in
2cm	¾in
2.5cm	1in
5cm	2in
6cm	2½in
8cm	3in
10cm	4in
13cm	5in
15cm	6in
18cm	7in
20cm	8in
23cm	9in
25cm	10in
28cm	11in
30cm	12in (1ft)

OVEN TEMPERATURES

These oven temperatures are only a guide for conventional ovens. For fan-forced ovens, check the manufacturer's manual.

	°C (CELSIUS)	°F (FAHRENHEIT)
Very slow	120	250
Slow	150	275-300
Moderately slow	160	325
Moderate	180	350-375
Moderately hot	200	400
Hot	220	425-450
Very hot	240	475

The imperial measurements used in these recipes are approximate only. Measurements for cake pans are approximate only.

INDEX